Introductory Bird Watching

The Complete
Beginner's Guide to Bird Watching

Leigh Watson

Published by Dr. Patrick Johnson, 2023

Introductory Bird Watching

The Complete Beginner's Guide to Bird Watching

Table of Contents

Legal Notices & Disclaimers

and unique perception of the information. As a result, no guarantees are made.

Without the publisher's written permission, you can't copy or move any part of this work or the files that go with it, whether electronically or in another way.

Introduction

Had you ever had a day where you had nothing to do? You know those moments when you're on the internet in a chat room and type, "I'm bored!" or when you're browsing through the TV channels and exclaim, "There are 250 channels, and there's nothing nice to watch!" Yes, you know what I'm talking about. Now that you have something to do on those so-called boring days, you can go bird watching.

Bird watching is an activity that has been practiced for many years. In fact, only gardening is currently America's second-fastest growing hobby, behind bird watching. Along with it, a completely new language has developed. People in the know also call bird watching "birding" and those who engage in it "birders."

All ages take pleasure in finding their local birds, viewing them in their natural habitat, and listening to the melodies they have to offer. Birds are often intriguing animals with a lot to teach anyone who takes the time to learn about them. Much can be discovered by observing where they roost, how they fly, and what they sing. We could even go so far as to say that observing birds can teach us about nature and the beauty that it contains.

"When I was hoeing in a village garden once, a sparrow briefly perched on my shoulder, and I felt more distinguished by that experience than I should have by any epaulette I could have worn."

~Thoreau, Henry David

You can go birding anywhere. All different species can be found in your neighborhood park, any forest, and even in your own garden!

Nobody is as familiar with the sights and sounds of nature as a bird watcher. A birder can tell you the specific bird by taking a quick look at a small cluster of darting black, yellow, and white feathers and adding a musical note that sounds like "chirp." They can do this without even knowing the overall species of the bird.

Birders must swiftly digest a vast amount of data on color patterns, call notes, and even the shapes of bills in order to distinguish among the 900+ species of birds found in the U.S. When they see a strange bird, they need to know what to focus on, taking note of its overall shape, how it glides through a shrub or tree, and the shape of its wings. Such sensory exercises aid in the development of excellent visual and hearing acuity in birders. In actuality, bird watchers are typically much more perceptive than the average individual.

The novice bird watcher might think that this is an impossible endeavor that they will never be able to complete. Even common species can be exceedingly difficult to identify, and many individuals give up before they even start.

Finding and identifying birds might happen in a single instance. Flashing up to the top of a bush is a little black bird. You take out your binoculars and begin leafing through your field manual. You take another look at the bird and turn a few pages back. Suddenly, the bird is gone, but a different one has appeared deeper in the bush. This page riffling and binocular lifting process begins again.

Birding can increase your awareness of the world's natural beauty and perhaps help you realize how swiftly that beauty is disappearing. Birding may lure you into a foreign country and give you the chance to take in as much of the clean air and stunning landscape as you can. But what matters most is that birding is just too much pleasure to pass up.

The kind of knowledge offered here is second nature to an experienced birder, yet it can take a beginning bird viewer several months of hard work to understand these concepts and procedures. Even with the information provided here, it will still take time and effort on your part to become one of the most tuned-in nature viewers.

We have made an effort to remove some of the mysticism around bird viewing and highlight the essentials, but patience and practice are equally crucial to bird watching as they are to sports, music, and other leisure hobbies. You shouldn't expect to identify all of those difficult birds on your first expedition or record 150 different species (although this will be possible later on). You must put effort into it.

This book is meant to assist you in moving past the difficult beginning. It is a crash course in the fundamentals of "birding," or watching birds. With this book's guidance, hopefully you'll be well on your way to a greater appreciation of the world around you, since birding concentrates on some of the most amazing creatures on the planet.

Like humans, birds are highly visual creatures. Some species of birds wear stunning combinations of yellow, blue, red, black, and green to make them clearer to the unaided eye. They also come in a wide variety of shapes and sizes, which adds to the enjoyment of bird watching.

You might discover that bird watching isn't just enjoyable but also educational. Birding gets you outside, provides exercise, challenges your thinking, and improves your observational abilities.

Read on and join us as we discuss introductory bird watching!

Watching Birds as a Hobby

People who are viewing or studying birds use the terms "bird watching" or "birding." Bird watching is an activity that can be done for business purposes, as a hobby, as a group activity to do with friends and family, or on your own.

Watching birds is not just for scientists.

The scientists who study birds are known as ornithologists. Their field of study is known as ornithology. They may employ similar methods and procedures as amateur bird watchers, but much more meticulously. Even though amateur bird watchers frequently know a lot about the birds that live on our planet, they are not scientists. They like seeing and hearing these incredible animals, but they leave the scientific research to the ornithologist.

Spring and fall are frequently the best times of year to go bird watching in many parts of the world because this is when the majority of bird species can be seen migrating. These birds often migrate from the northern hemisphere to the southern hemisphere in the fall to spend the winter.

Many bird watchers concur that the early morning hours are the best times to observe birds because at this time the birds are typically actively foraging for food. Due to the bird's active searching, it is simpler to observe and study them as subjects.

A person may also benefit from having specific knowledge about the bird's appearance, song or melody, behavior, and most likely habitat in order to be successful in their search to find birds for bird watching. To see the most variety of birds and be able to get close to the birds, it helps to have a lot of patience, be quiet, and be very stealthy.

Why do People Watch Birds?

Birds have long brought joy to people everywhere in the world because of their beauty and ability to fly. There are birds everywhere, and they are all unique. Birds are intriguing, lovely, and occasionally delightfully evasive.

They were historically regarded as bad omens. The ancient Romans thought that bird sounds and flights could predict the future.

Today's science continues to use birds as a sort of oracle. Bird population changes may be an indicator of the state of the ecosystem.

Another primal drive that is satisfied by birding is the desire for information. Birding is about learning new things. not just about the names of birds but also about their songs, behaviors, and relationships to the rest of nature. The successful application of knowledge is the ideal opportunity to indulge in a special human pleasure.

In fact, novice birders frequently have the opportunity to contribute significantly to science. Today, a large portion of what is known about birds in the field of ornithology comes from the observations of regular but devoted birders.

Some birds, like the bald eagle, the national bird of the United States, are indicator species. They predict the state of the environment. Understanding birds can help us design a healthier, more lasting relationship with nature.

Perhaps we watch birds because they are so easily available; they are typically there wherever we go, active when we are active and asleep when we are asleep. In our own backyards, we entice them with birdfeeders and birdhouses, as well as appropriate trees, shrubs, and water features. Birds obviously share our outdoor space more than any other creature, with the possible exception of insects. If we must go great distances and wait patiently for long periods of time in order to see a rare or elusive bird that makes it a treasure hunt.

We enjoy novelty and treasure hunts. Birds offer both. Despite the fact that many birds have extremely vast ranges, the birds in one nation tend to differ from those in another; even if you find the birds at home to be rather common, you will be delighted by unknown birds when you travel. You will see the same kind of bird in several places, but the actual birds will vary.

Birds are lovely. Their vivid colours serve as a companion to their sense of colour. Birds have variety of colours, from emerald to vermillion, and are just as stunning as flamboyant flower blossoms but usually more unexpected. We are delighted by the infinite diversity of patterns, shapes, and sizes. Even the common crow has a gorgeous gloss and an air of formality. Indeed, watching birds is a wonderful part of life. How could we not?

Bird watching is enjoyable! It gives you a good reason to step away from the screen and go outside into the elements. Need a compelling reason to get outside and take a stroll? Bring your binoculars with you. It is a healthy activity that just about everybody can appreciate. You don't require strong knees for skiing. You don't even need to be able to leave your own backyard. Individuals with low resources can enjoy birds with little to no effort thanks to bird feeders set up on window sills.

Birding is the ideal sport to play alone. Going outside alone to observe birds can be really enjoyable. Your thoughts become calmer. Your senses become more acute, and nature seems to become your buddy. Birding is an activity that appeals to a variety of moods and may be enjoyed alone or with friends.

However, be aware that birding can become obsessive. You can become fixated on certain unusual species that have been reported locally. You notice that you are rising earlier and earlier to squeeze in some birding time before work. As you start adding more bird-friendly plants, erecting feeders and bird baths, and limiting the use of toxic chemicals, you start to look at your landscaping in a completely new way.

As we've already mentioned, birds are interesting animals. If you've never seen them, just try to find a few minutes in the early morning light. As they glide over the sky, observe them. Play their morning songs for me. You can discover a lot of calm and wisdom in birds. How would you be able to truly enjoy these creatures if you hadn't seen them? It's time to start watching birds!

How to Begin Bird Watching

Anyone of any age can enjoy bird watching as a relaxing hobby and enjoyable pastime. The lovely sound of birds singing and chirping must have woken you up in the mornings. Wouldn't it be wonderful to see the bird creating the sounds in person?

Many people believe that in order to become a "birder," which is short for "bird watcher," you must be an expert. But this is not the case.

Try the following steps to begin bird watching:

1. Begin by listening to birds.

Go outside to your backyard garden, close your eyes, and pay special attention to the captivating sounds of nature. Your mind will filter out all other sounds when you concentrate on the chirping of birds, and you'll suddenly become aware of an amazing tune that you were previously unaware of.

Try to locate the source of the sounds by opening your eyes, then move toward those sounds. See if you can identify the bird that is singing throughout. See how close you can get before the bird becomes spooked and takes off.

You might now be wondering what the actual name of the bird you saw is.

2. Invest in some bird-watching gear.

There are steps you may take to draw birds to specific sections of your yard so that you can see them more clearly. In a particular region of your garden, you can create bird houses, bird baths, or bird feeders. This will draw in birds looking for food or water.

You will want a field guide in order to recognize the native species in your region. A field guide is essentially a book with bird images and identification advice. The best books for beginning birders in the United States are the "Peterson Field Guide to Eastern Birds" or the "Peterson Field Guide to Western Birds."

Because they are not very tame, wild birds are quickly frightened. You will therefore need to observe these birds from a distance. You will need a pair of binoculars to see these birds clearly. The best birders typically have the best binoculars, which allow them to recognize birds at a distance of 100 yards by their silhouette.

Additionally, wearing camouflage clothing can help you blend into your surroundings and ensure that you can approach the birds even closer without frightening them.

You'll need a diary to keep track of your bird sightings. It's useful to keep track of the various places, whether they were in your hometown, town, country, or while you were on vacation, where you saw a specific species. Some birders keep track of sightings by season and frequency. The "Birder's Diary" tool is useful for keeping track of your sightings.

3. Watch the birds during feeding time.

Fill your bird feeder with seeds, then sit back and watch the various species of birds that come to visit. Remember to take note of their size, colour, beak form, wing span, and flight patterns.

A useful method is to change the food to attract different species of birds. Many different birds, including cardinals and woodpeckers, are drawn to peanut butter. Cockatiels and songbirds both enjoy seeds. Use a range of seeds, berries, fruit, nuts, and sunflower seeds, and observe the various birds that each of these draws. Even planting the correct flowers can draw in animals like the hummingbird.

Another effective way to draw birds is with a birdbath. They frequently visit these for a drink or to take a bath during the humid summer months.

4. Join a club that studies birds.

Perhaps the best way to learn about bird watching is to join a bird watching organization and go bird watching with experienced birders.

These people will transfer knowledge that will significantly speed up the process of learning about this activity. To help you expand your knowledge, they will suggest the best websites, periodicals, and other publications.

The best way to increase your understanding of birds is to subscribe to a birding magazine. Subscribe to "Birdwatch" for UK birds and "Birder's World" or "Birding" for US birds.

The best way to meet knowledgeable birders is to get in touch with your neighborhood Audubon chapter or birding group. Most likely, a neighborhood club in your region arranges birding outings for visitors. Do a Google search and make a reservation for one of these journeys. You'll learn about fascinating environments in your area, fascinating species, and amazing insights into how seasoned birders conduct their business. Do not be hesitant to take notes, ask questions, or learn by doing.

Don't let the somewhat high learning curve of bird watching diminish the fun you get from it. You'll find it easier to discover birds, identify them, and record data if you tag along with knowledgeable birders.

Try to imitate what seasoned birders do by keeping an eye out for it.

5. Time

You must be aware that you can only see specific birds at specific longitudes and latitudes during specific seasons. Birds are masters of migration, and specific species can be found in various locations at various times of the year. It is best to consult with your local bird watching club for information on the bird species that live in your area all year.

Bird Watching Equipment

The best thing about bird watching is that you don't need many instruments to accomplish it well. A good set of binoculars, a field guide, a notebook, and a camera should be all you need to get started. Let's examine each component separately.

Binoculars

You need binoculars to see the birds more clearly. You'll soon learn an ironic fact. The best birders have the best binoculars, even if they can recognize a bird's silhouette from 100 yards away. Newcomers with a subpar pair of binoculars see a fuzzy ball of feathers but are unsure of what kind of bird it is. The price gap between a $59 pair of binoculars and a $900 pair is astounding.

The quality of a birding trip can be significantly impacted by the use of binoculars, which are a birder's eyes on the world. Good binoculars are essential for successful birding, whereas poor binoculars can cause missed birds and excruciating headaches from double vision, blurred images, and eye strain.

Binoculars are available in a wide variety of forms and designs, and they may be described as "roof prism," "tight focus," "armor coated," etc.

You don't need to spend a lot of time at first trying to understand this mysterious vocabulary. If you become obsessed with bird watching, you can eventually learn more about binoculars and upgrade to a better set. Depending on where you reside, you may expect to pay around $60 for a nice pair of binoculars.

There are a few straightforward guidelines to follow and inquiries to make when buying your first pair of binoculars.

1. Ensure that the power (or magnification) is at least seven times. The first number given in the numerical notation used to describe binoculars is the power. For instance, a "7 x 35" set of "glasses" will make things appear to be seven times as close together as they actually are. To see birds clearly, seven-power binoculars are about the bare minimum required. Some birders may find it challenging to maintain stability when using binoculars with 10 power or higher.

2. Check to see that the second number (35 for a pair of glasses that are "7 X 35") is at least five times as large as the power (e.g., "7 X 35," "8 X 40," etc.). The second number is the diameter, in millimeters, of the "objective"

lens, which is the large lens that confronts the subject of interest. The larger this lens is, the more light the binoculars will gather, and, as a result, the easier it will be to see features in low light or on a dull-colored bird.

3. Are the binoculars too hefty for you to carry and use continuously for at least two hours? Avoid developing a hunchback as a result of your binoculars acting as a yoke.

4. Can you bend the binoculars' barrels very easily? Spread the barrels as far as possible, then grasp onto just one of them to see if they are too flexible. The free barrel falls or slips out of the spread position. It should not at all.

5. Do the large objective lenses have a blue or purple tint when held a foot away? If they are, the lenses are colored. This coating improves the amount of light that really reaches your eyes while decreasing internal glare in the binoculars. Make sure the coatings on the lenses are free from any blemishes or scrapes.

6. Can you get the binoculars' barrels close enough together so that the image you see combines into a single, clear image inside of a single, perfect circle? The binoculars may be out of alignment, or the eyepieces may not be close enough to one another to accommodate your eyes if the image is not clear or solitary.

These two issues may cause headaches and eye strain.

7. Do you wear glasses with a prescription? Your binoculars should have rubber eyecups that can fold back if you do. This gives you a much wider field of view and enables you to place your eyeglasses up near the binoculars' eyepieces.

8. Can the binoculars clearly show an object that is only 20 feet away? You risk missing the sparrow or warbler that lurks in the neighboring bush since some binoculars do not focus on items this close.

9. Pay attention to a sign with big letters. Do the letters that are at the field of view's periphery appear to be as precise and well-formed as the characters that are in the middle? Poor binoculars frequently have image distortion toward the edge, which is similar to seeing through a fish-eye lens. Look for a pair with the least amount of distortion.

10. Are the letters and numbers visible when you focus on a license plate or small sign two blocks away? Choose a different pair if they aren't!

A broad list of things to keep in mind while purchasing binoculars:

• Avoid purchasing compact or pocket-sized binoculars as your primary pair for birding (usually 8 x 21 or 10 x 21). Although the compactness and weight are appealing, compact binoculars provide a lower-quality image than mid- or full-size binoculars, no matter how brilliant the optics are. Another disadvantage is that most compacts have a small field of view, which makes it extremely challenging to find and follow birds.

Avoid purchasing zoom binoculars. They are rated as substandard by experienced birders.

• Don't ask non-birders for advice on purchasing optics. Birders' needs are different from those of hikers, hunters, and boaters. Looking at birds is different from looking at other wildlife. For viewing an elephant or a cheetah over a savannah, pocket binoculars are perfect, but they are not appropriate for birding. Although they produce a clear, bright image, marine binoculars are too large and cumbersome to carry around all day.

• Prior to purchasing binoculars, try them out. Make sure they are at ease in your hands. Look through them to ensure that you have an unimpeded, clear view. Different models fit different people differently, and every instrument differs. Ensure that you have the option to exchange them when ordering by mail or online.

One thing about binoculars is that you don't always need to have the best lenses for watching birds. Any pair of binoculars is preferable to none at all. The important thing to keep in mind is that you'll need something to magnify the birds you'll be looking for. If you're serious about bird watching, pay attention to the advice provided above when purchasing binoculars. They will be very worth the cost!

Utilizing Your New Binoculars in Practice

It's crucial to adjust your binoculars before using them so that they account for the disparities in your two eyes' acuity. Take a lens cap and use it to cover the right objective lens. Then, using your binoculars' main focusing knob, look through the left lens and focus on an object that is 30 feet away.

After focusing on the target, switch the lens cover from the right lens to the left lens. Look at the same thing through the right lens, but avoid touching the main focusing wheel! Use the focusing ring on your binoculars' right eyepiece to alter the image if it is not as clear as it appeared through the left lens. Take note of where you have the right eyepiece's focus fixed. Your binoculars are now adjusted to your eyes and prepared for use.

Next, spend some time honing the hand-eye coordination you'll need to quickly identify birds. It's clear that most bird-watching is not like watching football. With bird watching, there is a lot more activity because everything is happening at a scale of one hundredth and moving one hundred times as quickly across an infinite area of space. Developing the skill of spotting birds with binoculars takes time for novice birders. The trick is to develop your ability to recognize birds with the unaided eye before raising your binoculars to your eyes without ever taking your eyes off the bird.

Find a quiet area in a nearby park and dedicate some time to practicing object identification with your binoculars. Set the binoculars' focus lever at first so that a target around 30 feet away is clearly visible. This is a good starting point from which to learn how to adjust the binoculars' focus.

Then start looking for birds with your unaided eye before using your binoculars to locate them. Simply follow the bird for a bit while lowering and raising your binoculars intermittently. Don't bother about bird identification just now. Simply observe what they are doing. You'll soon be able to spot and concentrate like an expert.

Field Guides

A field guide is what? A field guide is a small book filled with details about birds. It's the next best thing to having a knowledgeable birder by your side. It discusses the species, provides images of each, and instructs you on what characteristics of each bird to look for.

A field manual may provide some fantastic advice on what to look for when bird watching as well as tell you what kinds of birds may be in your specific location. It is crucial to have a field guide since, without one, you won't know what kinds of birds you will be observing. Typically, a field guide will run you $20.

Bird identification advice and photographs can be found in a field guide. The Peterson Field Guide to Eastern Birds or the Peterson Field Guide to Western Birds is the best book for beginning birders. You'll probably want the third edition of the National Geographic Field Guide to the Birds of North America once you become familiar with the birds in your area. We advise Peterson's First Guide: Birds for novice birders. It won't overwhelm you with too many options, and it describes 188 common and noticeable birds. You should also take a look at the brand-new Stokes Field Guides.

There has been a significant increase in the number of bird field guides published in recent years. The first field guide of its kind, The Birds of Eastern North America by Roger Tory Peterson, was used most frequently until the late 1960s. By making correct bird identification possible, this book effectively popularized bird watching.

However, there are now specialized field guides available for many parts of the nation (Texas even has its own field guide), as well as for certain bird species, such as hawks, gulls, shorebirds, ducks, and others. These specialized books may eventually find their way into a birding enthusiast's library. However, novices should only consider thorough manuals when selecting their first field guide.

It is best to start with a book that features paintings of birds rather than images when buying your first one. Paintings provide painters the freedom to incorporate all identifying characteristics (referred to as "field marks") that make a bird identifiable in each picture. Due to sunlight or the bird's location, pictures frequently fail to capture all of these characteristics. However, while examining the specifics of a bird's shape, photographic guides can be a helpful companion resource.

Once you've chosen your field guide, don't immediately start looking for birds because you'll really discover difficulties and aggravation there instead. Many field guides have spent more time collecting dust than aiding in the identification of birds because their owners failed to learn how to use them.

When you first receive your field guide, sit down and read the entire introduction. Next, take a look at some of the images and determine where certain common birds you are familiar with are positioned in the field guide (i.e., front, back, or middle).

If you want to develop into an enthusiastic outdoor birder, you should look for a book that is simple to carry and swiftly flick through. Portability is less crucial if you are more of a backyard birder who enjoys viewing local species at your bird feeders and birdbath.

Field Guide Structure

Many beginners have a tendency to spot a bird and then open their field guide to the middle pages right away. Then, after looking at the right ten pages and the left ten pages, they failed to locate the bird. Then they turn 20 pages to the right and 20 pages to the left without succeeding in finding the bird. They glance over a few more pages left and right before throwing the manual into the air in disgust and giving up the whole business.

This occurs because the user hasn't figured out how the bird species are organized in the field guide. It seems logical that they get frustrated.

Field guides are arranged according to a precise method that establishes where certain birds are located in the book, just as dictionaries and phone books are.

You wouldn't start anywhere in the middle if you were looking up the word "aardvark" in the dictionary, would you? Similar to this, if you see a bird that resembles a sparrow sitting on the ground, don't begin your search in the middle of a field guide because all sparrows are listed in the latter quarter of field guides.

Most manuals are generally arranged in "phylogenetic order." According to similarities in their current appearance, living things—not just birds—have most likely developed from a common ancestor according to phylogenetic order, which is how scientists describe all living things.

You can read your field guide to find out more about this sorting method. The idea is that in a field guide, birds with comparable physical characteristics are found quite closely together. There aren't any sparrows or loons facing a warbler on the same page as hawks. All sparrows, loons, warblers, hawks, and even gulls and blackbirds are spread out over a large number of pages.

There are five fundamental levels of classification that all birds fall under. The most specific degree of classification is used when referring to a group of 15 blue jays as belonging to the same "species" of birds.

Similar species are categorized into "genus," different genera are categorized into "families," different families are categorized into "orders" of birds, and all orders are categorized into just one "class." This is the "Aves" class, which is Latin for all birds. As you might expect, species in the same genus are more closely related to one another and resemble one another than species in other genera. In a similar vein, families arranged in the same order tend to be more similar to one another than families arranged in different orders.

Most field guides for North America contain between 800 and 900 species, which are classified into over 300 genera, 74 families, and just 20 different orders (guides for only eastern or western North America have around half as many species).

The family is the most practical and reasonable level of classification for a beginner birder to concentrate on. There are simply too many genera and species for a beginner to understand readily, and the range of identification within a certain order is too wide to be difficult. More importantly, you will develop the qualities of observation that define a good birder by becoming familiar with the basic size, shape, and look of the various bird groups.

In actuality, you probably know more about some of the families than you think. For instance, if you can identify a laughing gull, you already have a good idea of the sizes and shapes of all gulls. Similar to how knowing how a cardinal looks helps you learn more about other members of this family, such as buntings and grosbeaks, you also learn that they have very thick, pointed bills.

Even if you have no prior knowledge of the local birds, you can go anywhere on the globe and instantly find yourself head and shoulders above non-birders in terms of identification skills if you have the ability to distinguish the forms of the major bird families.

Therefore, when you first get your field guide, take some time to look at how it is organized and how it groups bird families. Utilize tags or sticky notes to divide your guide into four sections. The first quarter will consist of the large land bird families (all in the order "Passeriformes," also known as the "passerines" or "perching birds"), the second quarter the large land bird families (ending with the woodpeckers), and the final two quarters the tiny land bird families.

Continue looking for common species that you already know and use them as a reference to learn the traits shared by other species in the same family. Remember that you should start birding with your head and not by dashing around in search of elusive thrushes and perplexing fall warblers. Take a casual, not frenetic, approach when observing unfamiliar species. With your spyglasses and reliable field guide in hand, you can now start getting to know all of those flitting bundles of feathers.

Notebook

This doesn't need to be anything elaborate. We advise using something smaller than the typical 8 x 11 size. Carry something that is manageable and can be kept on your person without becoming overbearing.

What would you like to write down in your notebook? The types of birds you've seen, where you saw them, how they seemed and sounded, etc. When you make these observations as soon as you notice (or hear) them, you will be able to reflect on your experience more effectively in the future.

Camera

Although this isn't always thought of as a necessary piece of gear for bird viewing, we believe it should be. If you come across a particularly lovely type of bird and want to record it for later study, you may either rely on your memory or just take a picture.

The majority of the globe is now going digital. Get a digital camera with the most pixels possible so you can take the best possible photographs. Make sure your camera has a zoom lens so you can get "up close and personal" with your lovely feathered companions. Please turn off the flash as well. Nothing can scare a bird away faster than a camera flash!

You can also conduct a more thorough investigation of the birds you observe once you get home if you have images of the species you see. You can read your field guide more thoroughly and record the precise birds you encountered on your journey with images.

And consider the photo album you could make! Beautiful!

Another thing?

Most seasoned bird watchers strongly advise wearing a hat to protect your head from the sun and make you less noticeable. Any old thing will work. Birding is not a runway show. But the hat should protect your eyes and not get in the way of using your binoculars.

A birding vest is also helpful. You can store your field guide, binoculars, pen, notebook, and possibly some insect repellant in the pockets. You'll be prepared to quickly grab the vest and have everything you need for bird viewing if you hang it near the door.

Last but not least, you should wear neutral-colored clothing, not white, when birding. The last thing you want to do is draw attention to yourself while you're viewing normally timid animals in brightly coloured attire.

Now that you are equipped, let's first discuss some bird-watching guidelines and etiquette.

The Ideal Guidelines for Bird Watching

Wherever we go, there are some laws we must abide by, and when you go bird watching, there are similar laws you must follow. These are designed to protect both the birds and other bird watchers.

The first and most important rule is to treat birds with respect. Yes, they are attractive to look at, but think for a moment about whether you are the one being observed. Would you like that to occur to you? Although they are almost never caged as in a zoo, I bet you can picture the paparazzi following your every move.

The second guideline for bird viewing is not to approach the birds too closely. You are currently in their territory, where these animals return year after year to the same spot like clockwork. They will never again return to this location if you harm them or their surroundings, and you won't ever see them again.

The third guideline for bird viewing is to obey the law. The law protects birds, especially those that are in danger of extinction. If you encounter a bird that isn't in a national park but rather on someone else's land, you should also ask the owner if you can enter; otherwise, you risk being detained for trespassing.

Knowing the birds is the fourth guideline for successful bird viewing. In addition, there are 20 different bird families in the world. Don't assume for a second that visiting a national park would allow you to see all of them because they live in various conditions and ecosystems. Find out what birds are local to the area so you don't waste all of that effort. Your ability to recognize these birds will increase if you are aware of what is nearby.

The alternative is to purchase a guidebook from the park staff. Remember that the folks who are doing the research have already finished it, so once you have a copy, all you need to do is mark the birds you were able to see on your field trip with a pen or pencil.

Most of the time, just by listening to or observing the bird, you will be able to identify it. It should take you a little bit longer to interpret their behavior, colour, silhouette, and voice if you are new to this activity. All things considered, certain birds can appear to be the same when viewed through binoculars or a scope.

Following these four simple rules will ensure that you have a good time bird watching. Don't be concerned if you only see a few of the birds you know live in the area; you can always return the following week to try again.

There are now more people than ever who like observing birds. While some begin looking out their windows, anyone who wants to see other species up close will visit national parks not just in the states and nations where they reside but also elsewhere.

Wherever you go, keep in mind that you are essentially a visitor in their territory and that it is most appropriate to have things that way. Report it if you see anything strange about their behavior, as this is how you show concern for the birds' welfare.

Etiquettes for Bird Watching

With your knowledge and excitement in hand, you are now prepared to enter the field and add dozens of new species to your notebook. But don't let your enthusiasm get in the way of good birding manners.

Remember to tread lightly and respect borders because you will be entering the territory of several birds in order to find them.

Never forget the value of stillness. Birds are quite perceptive, and they often become aware of your presence before you even get a chance to see them. Walk as quietly as you can and whisper, whether you're alone or with a group. Take direction from the leader, who may signal for silence as the group draws near a bird. Walking quietly will be helpful when listening for bird calls.

A potential or active nesting area requires special caution. Birds already struggle to compete with one another for mates and territory; human meddling adds to their stress.

Make sure you aren't intruding on someone else's property. Some bird sanctuaries are situated on private property, whose owners might not appreciate outsiders with binoculars wandering about their yard. Make sure you have permission before you go.

Don't act like a spy! Be careful not to point your binoculars at other people or their houses.

While some birders prefer to be alone, others love birding in groups and sharing their discoveries. Don't be shy if you're new to birding; someone in the group who is more experienced will be happy to share their expertise and sightings with you.

Most importantly, have fun! Be less focused on discovering that rare bird or spotting more species than you were last month. Birding is intended to be educational as well as enjoyable.

We feel it's vital to quote the "Principles of Birding Ethics" from the American Birding Association here:

PRINCIPLES OF BIRDING ETHICS OF THE AMERICAN BIRDING ASSOCIATION

Anyone who appreciates birds and bird watching must always respect wildlife, their surroundings, and other people's rights. The interests of the birds and their surroundings come first in any disagreement between birders and the birds.

Bidding Ethics Code

1. Advocate for the protection of birds and their environment.

1(a): Encourage the preservation of critical bird habitat.

1(b): Use restraint and caution when watching, photographing, recording sound, or filming birds to prevent stressing them or putting them in danger.

Limit the use of recordings and other methods to attract birds, and never use these methods in heavily birded areas or to attract any species that is threatened, endangered, of special concern, or that is uncommon in your area. Also, keep a safe distance from nests, nesting colonies, roosts, display areas, and important feeding sites. If there is a need for prolonged observation, photography, filming, or recording in such sensitive regions, try to use a blind or hide and take advantage of the available natural cover.

For cinematography or photography, use artificial light sparingly, especially for close-ups.

1(c) Before announcing the presence of a rare bird, consider the possibility of disruption to the bird, its surroundings, and other local residents. Only proceed if access can be restricted, disturbance can be kept to a minimum, and permission has been acquired from private landowners. Only the appropriate conservation authorities should be informed of the locations of uncommon breeding birds.

1(d) Remain on routes, trails, and roads where they are present; otherwise, cause as little disruption to the habitat as possible.

2. Respect the law and other people's rights.

2(a): You must obtain the owner's express consent before entering private property.

2(b) Comply with all laws, rules, and ordinances that apply both at home and abroad on the use of highways and public spaces.

2(c): Always be courteous when interacting with others. Your exemplary conduct will win you friends among both birders and non-birders.

3. Ensure the safety of feeders, nesting structures, and other man-made bird settings.

3(a): Keep food, water, and dispensers clean and free of decay or disease. Inclement weather necessitates constant bird feeding.

3(b): Maintain and clean nest structures on a regular basis.

3(c) When luring birds to a location, make sure they are not in danger of being eaten by cats or other domestic animals, or of being injured by man-made hazards.

4. Group birding, whether planned or unplanned, calls for special consideration.

Each member of the group has responsibilities as a group member in addition to the duties outlined in Items #1 and #2.

4(a): Respect your fellow birders' interests, rights, and abilities as well as those of those engaging in other lawful outdoor activities. Share your expertise without restriction, barring situations where code 1(c) is relevant. Be very beneficial to novice birders.

4(b): Evaluate the situation if you see unethical bird watching activity and take appropriate action if you feel it is necessary. When intervening, let the person(s) know that what they are doing is improper and make reasonable efforts to get it stopped. If the behavior persists, note it and let the appropriate people or organizations know.

Group leader duties for both amateur and expert outings and tours

4(c) Be an example of an ethical member of the organization. Instruct with words and examples.

4(d): Keep groups to a size that minimizes their influence on the environment and doesn't obstruct other people from using the same space.

4(e): Assure that everyone in the group is aware of and adheres to this code.

4(f): Find out and let the group know about any unique circumstances that may apply to the places being visited (such as the fact that no recorders are allowed).

4(g): Recognize that professional tour operators have a special obligation to prioritize bird welfare and public education over their own financial interests. Leaders should ideally keep track of tour sightings, record unexpected events, and submit records to the appropriate organizations.

Please abide by this code, disseminate it, and teach others how to do so.

Even though it may seem monotonous, it is worth repeating for the sake of fellow bird watchers as well as the birds we are viewing!

You have the necessary tools and are aware of what you should and should not do. Now let's go look for some birds!

How to Pick the Right Hat for Bird Watching

Observing birds is such a relaxing activity. Many people engage in bird watching not only to see and study their favorite species but also as a way to decompress. According to studies, birdwatchers exhibit fewer indicators of pressure and stress than other people to those who occupy the space and watch TV or fiddle with their computers. In comparison to his or her peers, the individual who engages in bird watching benefits more from being outdoors and connecting with nature. If you have a sedentary indoor lifestyle, engaging in some bird watching will substantially assist you in maintaining your physical and mental health.

If you want to go bird watching, you will need at least two essential items. You will need binoculars first, and then you will need a cap. A bird-watching hat is just as crucial as binoculars because it will shield you from the sun's heat. Be aware that exposure to the direct heat of the sun is now regarded as dangerous due to the damage done to your planet's ozone layer. Because occurrences of skin cancer caused by the sun's harmful UV rays have significantly increased in recent years, we should never take anything for granted when we go outside in the sun. No matter how infrequently we are exposed to the sun, you still need to take precautions to avoid being directly exposed to it.

You must take the hat's size, shape, and colour into consideration while selecting one for bird viewing. Over such delicate-looking hats, pick a hat with a wide brim. Wide-brimmed hats that shade your face are an efficient way to shield it from the harmful effects of the sun. When compared to bird-watching hats made of leather and other materials, hats made of thick cotton can be far cooler. Additionally, hats made of cloth are simpler to maintain than those that are constructed of harder materials. Be aware that your hat's hard materials may be somewhat uncomfortable, especially if you're trying to get a better view of your favorite bird.

Your bird viewing attire's colour is crucial. While wearing brightly coloured bird-watching hats can be rather lovely, they aren't really appropriate for the activity. Brightly coloured clothing draws attention away from your hiding area. Try some of those earth-colored hats instead of using ones with flashy colours. When you want to blend in with the bushes, brown bird-watching hats in particular are really helpful.

Where to Look For Birds

The wonderful thing about birding is that you can do it almost everywhere! You can go to your neighborhood park and find some excellent examples there. Traveling will give you a new appreciation for the sounds of birds and the things you may see. Even in your own backyard, you can watch birds! Later on in this book, we'll talk more about backyard birding.

You must be aware of local expectations. This information can be found on bird checklists for your area. Many state and national parks close to you have bird sighting checklists. There are several websites that include checklists for every country in the world as well as every state and province in the United States and Canada! Other fantastic birdwatching websites can be found online.

Discover which habitats each species of bird prefers. Do they prefer to spend their time on the ground, in a lake, or at the top of a tree? You should become familiar with the bird melodies in your yard. Learn the songs of other birds in your region of the country afterwards. You will frequently hear a bird before seeing it.

You might like to associate with some other birders. Birders are really helpful and friendly.

They are always eager to impart their knowledge. We were all newbies once. Start by contacting your neighborhood Audubon Society, nature centre, parks commission, or bird club. If all else fails, take your binoculars to the park. Someone is bound to start a discussion with you, and they might introduce you to an entirely new group of birding companions.

Take a tour or trip for birdwatching. Sometimes, local bird tours are advertised in the newspapers. These are frequently led by local Audubon members or park rangers. You should also dial your local Rare Bird Alert phone line to learn more about local excursions.

They frequently announce planned field trips after listing the uncommon birds that have been spotted in the vicinity. The trips could take all day or only one morning. These outings are frequently cost-free. You might also want to go on a tour with a qualified guide. Although they are paid for their services, tour guides are well worth the money. Birding trips can take you anywhere in the world.

Not always do birds hang out in upscale locations; sewage ponds are a favorite. But you don't have to start there. Take a stroll by a brook, across a meadow, along a trail, or along the shore. Birds can be seen throughout the journey.

One tip: Stay away from wooded areas where birds hide themselves. It's best to find open spaces with trees or bushes. Remember to visit the zoo. It probably has a pond with ducks and other waterfowl, and they are accustomed to seeing people.

Plan a trip that includes time for birding. Wherever you go, research the best places for bird watching beforehand and plan your vacation accordingly. The articles by amateur birders in the bimonthly journal Bird Watcher's Digest describe the pleasures of this sport. The publication offers destinations that cater to birders.

It wouldn't be a sport if birds were always visible on branches. Otherwise, it wouldn't be a sport. From the ground to small shrubs, and from tree trunks to the tops of skyscrapers, species can be found at several eye levels. Read about the types of habitat that birds like for feeding, mating, and raising young once you are aware of which species are present in your area and when. The easier it is to see birds, the more likely it is that you have birdfeeders, birdhouses, and birdbaths in your yard.

Depending on the species, there are specific times of day when birds are more active than others. The best time to see the majority of birds is typically early in the morning; the evening is less fruitful unless you're looking for nocturnal species, like owls. Pay attention to the season as well. It's easy to identify birds that travel long distances and stop in your area for a rest during the spring and fall migrations.

How can you identify the birds you observe now that you have the necessary tools and knowledge?

How to Identify Birds

There are hundreds of different bird species in the world. You most likely won't be able to name every single bird you see. However, equipped with some fundamental knowledge, you can probably narrow down the list and discover that you might have a species worth researching.

What should you look for when recognizing birds? Developing your visual recognition skills takes time and perseverance. Some bird species are much simpler to positively identify than others.

First and foremost, don't make bird identification difficult for yourself. Two general guidelines to keep in mind throughout your first few months of bird watching are as follows:

Before you attempt to identify anything,

1) Exclude as many species as you can from consideration, and

2) Make sure the bird is most likely a species that is native to your area and not some unusual exotic that blew in from a thousand miles away.

One of the simplest ways to exclude birds is to look through your field guide and mark any that don't generally occur in your area with an "X." Place these aside for the time being.

By doing this, you significantly lower the number of birds you have to worry about identifying from the 900 in your book to the 300 or so that are frequently seen in your area!

By the way, don't bother marking up your field guide. The best companion you can have when exploring alone is a field guide that has been specifically tailored to your needs. Just be sure to use permanent ink or a pencil so that the text won't smear if you periodically drop the book in the mud or leave it out in the rain.

Consider the time of year the bird might be present in your area as another method of narrowing down your options. This kind of data is displayed on the range maps that come with field guides. Even some novices might find it helpful to add coloured dots next to the birds in their field guides.

Put a red dot next to birds that are year-round residents, a blue dot next to birds that only come during the winter, a green dot next to birds that only visit during the summer, and a black dot next to birds that only pass through during migration, for instance.

IDENTIFICATION CLUES

The way some birds skulk around, you'd think they were embarrassed by their beautiful colours and didn't want anyone to recognize them. Undeniably, this is the case, as they must somehow avoid predators from above and below. They frequently move quickly and just give us a glance. However, by using the crucial identification cues described here, you will be able to identify even the most elusive bird.

There are five simple hints you may listen for and look for to help you answer the bird identification puzzle:

1) Bird's shape;

2) Its coloration and plumage;

3) Its behavior;

4) Its preferred habitats; and

5) Its sound.

Although this may seem like a huge amount of data to compile, you usually only need one or two of these hints to identify a bird.

Identifying a bird can sometimes be as simple as knowing which hint to look for first when you spot one that doesn't fit the norm.

You will be able to identify the key hints with more assurance and ease as your birding skills advance.

Size and Shape: Silhouette

As you become more familiar with your field guide, you will be able to easily classify the majority of birds into families based solely on their silhouettes (remember, each family has a distinct form and size).

This will immediately give you an advantage over the ordinary observer since you have already limited the list of possible birds by classifying the bird you see into a certain family. You could only be spotting 15 or so birds, those belonging to the family of birds you have identified, out of the 900 listed in your field guide. As was already indicated, you can then eliminate any species in the family that don't naturally appear in your area during that season.

You may still perform this in the worst lighting situations, such as when birds are backlit, in low light, or in the shadows. It is irrelevant. The general shape has not changed. Many bird species can even be distinguished by a bird's shape.

Of course, initially achieving this achievement won't be simple. You must learn to take meticulous notice of every aspect of a bird's shape. Is the bird big or little, with short legs or long legs, crested or not, fat or slender and elegant, and with short or long tails? Record every detail in your field journal.

Another very useful hint that is obvious from a silhouette is the design of a bird's bill. The bills of cardinals, finches, and sparrows are small and conical. To deal with dead wood, woodpeckers have bills that resemble chisels. On the other hand, hawks, eagles, and falcons have sharp, hooked bills that quickly consume meat. Shorebirds have long, narrow bills for exploring the sand at various depths.

The beak is a dead giveaway. It indicates the bird's feeding habits, such as whether it cracks seeds (short, thick beak), drills for grubs (long, pointed beak), takes things off leaves (short, thin beak), and so on. Your bird guide can help you recognize different beak shapes.

Size is another crucial field indicator, and field guides do include the size of the birds next to their photos. However, these statistics aren't much use if you don't already have some sort of scale in mind. Many birders use a mental connection of three well-known birds with three general size classes as their "ruler" when they are out in the field.

A house sparrow measures 5 to 6 inches in length, a northern mockingbird measures 9 to 11 inches, and an American crow measures 17 to 21 inches. Now that you can describe any bird's size in terms like "bigger than a crow" or "smaller than a sparrow," you have an immediate picture of what it is likely to be. If you associate each of these three species with 5, 10, and 20-inch size classes, you will also have an immediate frame of reference for your field guide.

Plumage

Many people are drawn to bird watching because they enjoy admiring the beautiful colours of the plumage. "Field marks" are the distinctive plumage cues that distinguish different species. These consist of a variety of features, such as breast spots, wing bars (thin lines along the wings), eye rings (circles around the eyes), eyebrows (lines over the eyes), eye lines (lines through the eyes), and many more.

Some field markings can be better observed when a bird is in flight. With decent binoculars and keen vision, a soaring northern harrier may be distinguished from almost a mile away thanks to its dazzling white rump patch.

Some bird families can be divided into even smaller groups based on one or two straightforward field markings. For instance, there is a roughly equal distribution of warblers with and without wing bars. So, if you see a bird that resembles a warbler, take a quick look to see if it has wing bars. On the other hand, sparrows can be divided into two smaller groups according to whether or not their breasts are streaked. Search for other, more general distinctions for other families.

Behavior

One of the best indicators of a bird's identification is how it behaves, whether in flight, while foraging, or in general.

Crows and jays are "gregarious," crows and hawks are "serious," while cuckoos are, well, not really. Woodpeckers scale the sides of tree trunks in pursuit of grubs, much like a lineman would do with a telephone pole.

On the other hand, flycatchers wouldn't attempt to climb a tree trunk if their lives depended on it. They are usually found sitting up straight on an exposed perch. They quickly dash from their perch when they spot a beetle cruising within range, snag the meal, and then return to that perch or one close by.

As do mockingbirds, catbirds, and brown thrashers, finches spend a lot of time on the ground looking for fallen seeds. Some wading birds are very energetic foragers who chase their prey around in shallow waterways, such as snowy egrets and reddish egrets.

Other wading birds, like great blue herons, are less impulsive and hunt slowly and covertly.

Even the way a bird holds its tail gives some hints as to what species or family it may belong to. Wrens frequently bounce from side to side while holding their tails in a cocked position.

Louisiana water thrushes and spotted sandpipers bounce their tails and rump quickly up and down, as if performing a chic dance move. Certain thrushes and flycatchers, on the other hand, move their tails in a wave-like pattern frequently but slowly.

Some birds can even be recognized simply by the way they fly. The majority of finches and woodpeckers fly in an undulating rhythm, fluttering their wings briefly before tucking them under for a brief rest.

The buteos, or flying hawks, are one group of raptors that circle the sky while hanging from their outstretched wings. The majority of falcons are another group of raptors that frequently hover. Another species of bird, known as accipiters or bird hawks, often flies in a straight line while alternately flapping and floating.

Habitat

Even if a range map indicates that a certain bird appears in your area, this does not necessarily mean that it will be widespread wherever you go. Birds separate themselves according to habitat type and can occasionally be very particular about where they choose to live.

Ducks and wading birds, for instance, prefer wet habitats over arid uplands. Pine warblers and brown-headed nuthatches like pinewoods and are less frequent in places with significant populations of oaks, hickories, and other deciduous trees.

Beginner bird watchers typically need to spend a lot of time in the field before they can associate certain species with various types of habitat. You should create a key to the ecosystems you frequently visit and keep a record of the different species you see.

Use phrases like salt and freshwater marsh, pinelands, deciduous woodland, seaside, urban region, farm and pastureland, etc. to keep the habitat key basic at the beginning. Then expand on this as you learn to differentiate between the many habitat types.

After you have a sense of where the birds are, you can add acronyms such as "SM" (for saltwater marsh), "PW" (for pinewoods), and

"FP" (for farm and pasture) next to the photographs of birds in your field guide. Most field guides really provide this information in the textual description, but this condensed system may make it easier for you to recall the environments where each species is found.

Voice:

Birds have distinctive songs and calls, and voice is frequently all that is required to identify many of the birds you come across. When birds tried to communicate, there would be a lot of confusion if each species didn't have a readily recognizable call or song. Just as you can tell that Uncle Bob and not Aunt Edith are on the other end of the phone, so too can you learn to recognize the many bird voices.

When trying to learn bird vocalizations, listening to recordings is a huge assistance. Many are currently available on CD and cassette. They are also available online.

No matter how many recordings you listen to, going out into the field is still the best option. There is something about the link between voice and bird that aids in resolving both in memory. Furthermore, because bird vocalizations are so complex, no collection of recordings can hope to capture the full range and geographic differences that can be heard in nature.

Keep track of all of these details in your notebook while you observe the bird, noting its traits. As much as you can, keep watching. While your description is still fresh, write it down. Next, check your field guide for a more thorough identification.

In general, when attempting to identify the birds you observe, you should try to keep the following things in mind:

Start by concentrating on those groupings that are both common and unusual, and when you come across an unidentified species, take a visual inventory of its distinctive features. How big is it?

What is the body's shape? Whether it wades, hops, waddles, or walks? Observe the beak's form. Is it broad, stalky, flat, long, narrow, or hooked? Is the head covered with a crest? The tail may extend beyond the body. Is the tip square, forked, fan-shaped, or round?

Take a comprehensive inventory of the bird's hues. Look at the head, wings, and tail in particular. One of the most important characteristics that distinguishes ducks in flight is the colour of the speculum, or back edge, of the wing.

Take notice of the bird's behavior whenever it moves. This is frequently just as distinctive as its outward appearance. How does it maintain its tail? Is it located on the ground, atop trees, or in the skies?

Does it hold its body horizontally or upright while perched? Does it use its tail to support itself, as woodpeckers do? Does it tend to climb up or down the tree if it climbs along the trunk?

If it lives in or near the water, pay attention to how it swims. Does it dive entirely underwater or only dip its bill into the water while leaving its tail above the surface? Does it jump straight into the air as it takes off, or does it need a long runway to become airborne? Take notice of how long its legs are if it wades. Does it quickly rush along the shoreline while probing with its beak, or does it stalk slowly like a heron? Does it teeter like a spotted sandpiper or bob up and down like a dipper?

Does it maintain a steady beat while in the air, or does it undulate like a woodpecker? Does it typically fly straight ahead or does it undertake aerial maneuvers similar to a swallow? How quickly do its wings beat? Is it alone or part of a flock?

Additionally, noting the habitat and season may help identify a bird, or at the very least help differentiate between two species that are similar. Typically migratory, birds can be seen in big flocks on open water in the fall and spring. Understanding their habitat and annual cycles can frequently serve as the final crucial component in identification.

Determine whether it was eating nectar, fruit, insects, seeds, or other things if it was.

Other considerations when recognizing birds include:

• Color is not trustworthy, but it is what you notice first. The colour of a bird can change significantly depending on the type of lighting. Therefore, don't rely just on colour when attempting to identify the bird in a guide.

• Verify the range. You might think you've found the bird, but double-check to make sure it's there. Beginner birders make incredible discoveries, often finding the one and only instance of a species in that area. Your birding guide should provide range information for several species. Ensure that your bird belongs.

Don't rely solely on sound to locate a bird. They practice ventriloquism. And don't use your binoculars to scan the treetops. Instead, keep an eye out for movement before aiming your binoculars. Keep trying, even if you've managed to catch one of those annoying, fluttering warbler species. You'll obtain it.

• If you simply can't see it, forget about it. Keep in mind this rule: Any bird you missed seeing was a robin.

Don't forget to pay close attention to the bird's song. This could be the key to figuring out what kind of bird you have seen.

Bird Watching Using Your Ears

"A bird doesn't sing since it already knows the answer. Because it has a song, it sings.

~ Chinese saying

A bird's song can be soothing music or a shrill irritant. You can use its melody to determine what kind of bird it is and where to look for it in your field guide. You only need to listen to their music. Every kind of bird has its own distinct call, and you can recognize the different species just as simply by their shape or colour.

True, there are advantages to birding by ear. You can do it in the dark, which is useful for spotting owls while camping. The sound of a barred owl, for instance, is entirely different from any other sound you hear at night.

Often, a bird that is concealed by dense summer foliage will sing out its identity for everyone who has ears to hear. Although you can only see with your eyes in the direction you happen to be facing, you can hear in all directions simultaneously, allowing you to recognize a bird by its song even when it is behind you.

We humans experience the world differently than the majority of other organisms on earth. For instance, your dog just uses his nose to interact with the outside world, whereas our sense of smell is insignificant in comparison. Even trying to conceive what sensory sensations bats, insects, frogs, or fish would have is tough.

On the other hand, since sight and hearing are a bird's strongest senses, they have developed ways to communicate and identify their own species via signals based on those two senses. We can easily appreciate the wonderful differences in colour and shape that birds embody because we are also beings of sight and sound, and we can also recognize the sounds that are so vital to their existence.

As you learn to identify bird songs, you will enter a completely new realm of bird watching. You'll probably find yourself entranced by the bird outside your window's sing-song voice. and identify birds you didn't know you had nearby.

Get yourself a field guide to bird songs. To learn what birds sound like, just as you need a book with images to show you what they look like, you need recordings. Thankfully, there are now a number of good tapes and CDs of bird songs available. Additionally, there are several great online sources for bird songs. Learn these songs and introduce yourself to a brand-new world of bird watching!

Describe a bird's song to yourself in words when you hear it. Each note of the Northern Cardinal's song is a sluggish, downward slurp, and the White-breasted Nuthatch's "Yenk, yenk, yenk" song has a nasal quality. The blue jay's cry occasionally sounds loud and harsh, as if the bird were yelling "Thief!" Making a mental note of such details enables you to identify the bird when you hear it again.

Include an English phrase in the song, such as "Peter, Peter, Peter" for the tufted titmouse. You will be reminded of the song's rhythm, tempo, or pitch by the words.

It's best when you can match your own words to a bird's song, but feel free to use catchy lines that others have come up with. It's difficult to top the olive-sided flycatcher's call of "Quick, three beers!" and the ovenbird's call of "Teacher, teacher, TEACHER."

Once you give a bird's song words, you will always remember the melody. Chicago may no longer just refer to an Illinois city; instead, it may refer to the sound of the unusual bird you discovered the previous week.

Make a point of listening in the morning after you've gotten to know a few tunes. Many birds sing in the hour before morning. The chorus is beautiful to hear as a whole, but it's also fun to pick out and recognize the many voices in the choir. Some birds sing throughout the day, but you'll hear 100 times as much bird singing in the morning as you will in the middle of the day.

You can hear more birds with your ears than with your eyes at any time of year. Why not try it tomorrow morning? To hear the birds singing when you first wake up, sleep with a window open. Try to distinguish one song from the others if you are unsure of what they are. Even though the singer may continue to be a mystery to you for some time, it will act as your inspiration to develop your ability to "see with your ears."

To find birds, you don't necessarily need to travel. Many different types of birds can be drawn to your house, right in your own backyard. What could be more enjoyable than relaxing on your porch and taking up bird-watching in the comfort of your own home?

Technological Bird Watching

Modern tools and equipment are widely available and are of real value to bird watchers who want to get the most out of their encounters. Many people will have their own favorite and preferred methods of learning about birds, sharing that information with other bird watchers, or even documenting their discoveries so they can be shared with others. While some of the techniques used aren't particularly suitable for bird-watching excursions, all of them can be useful tools in the toolbox of any bird viewer, whether they are ardent enthusiasts or perhaps casual observers of local species. Here are a few items that could be helpful to any bird watcher or inspire you to become one!

Common Equipments

Binoculars, a spotting scope with a solid tripod, and one (or more!) field guides unique to the area they are based in or visiting are essential items for many bird watchers. These tools can be conveniently packed and transported on a bird watcher's person in a large bag or case. They are required for the distant observation of many bird species. They are simple to bring along on bird-watching excursions, and having reliable gear on hand while visiting a new place makes the entire experience just a little bit smoother and more pleasurable. Although everyone has a favorite pair of binoculars, several are designed specifically for the activity.

Sounds

One part of watching that isn't conveyed by the hobby's name and frequently astounds people when they learn about it is what may be referred to as "bird listening." Recognizing bird calls and other noises is an important aspect of bird watching. The location and identification of various varieties and even genders of birds can be made easier with the help of sound information. Because of advances in sound technology and the non-linear nature of digital storage, you can select and replay any desired individual sound while bird watching.

Photography

Taking pictures has always been a part of bird watching, and almost everyone has a camera that would be perfect for taking pictures while on bird watching tours. In the past, the price of high-quality cameras and telescopic lenses frequently made this a specialized area of bird watching. However, this has now become a much more popular component of the pastime as a result of digital cameras becoming more popular, which are frequently used in conjunction with spotting scopes. The ability of smaller digital versions to record not only sounds and likenesses but also bird flight patterns has made video cameras a significantly larger component of bird watching excursions and tours.

Remote Bird Watching

While many will argue that there is no appropriate replacement for in-person viewing excursions, these new technologies are enabling bird watching to take place online, using robotic camera deployments in strategic locations and distant animal habitats. These methods are currently being used in an effort to capture the rare ivory-billed woodpecker in its original form.

Garden Bird Watching

Finding songbird nests in the backyard is one of the happiest and most cherished memories of childhood. People of all ages are captivated by the unusual, mud-lined nests of robins and their exquisite blue eggs. The nesting habits of common birds like house wrens, cardinals, chickadees, and others can also inspire a lifetime interest in the natural world.

As you come to appreciate the beauty of the birdlife in the area around your house, you might want to enhance the "habitat" in your yard to attract more birds. You may draw birds to your yard by planting a variety of trees, shrubs, and flowers, as well as bird feeders, nest boxes, and bird baths. These can offer suitable nesting locations, winter protection, cover from predators, and year-round access to natural food sources.

There are a few different ways to attract various bird species to your yard. These could involve putting out a bird bath, building a bird feeder, or planting particular flowers.

By providing appropriate food, water, and habitats for wild birds as well as limiting the use of pesticides, you can engage in backyard birding and entice birds to your yard. Bushes and tall hedges offer perches, protection from predators, and a haven for insects that make excellent bird food. Hummingbirds are also attracted to vibrant blooms.

It doesn't matter if you live in an apartment, townhouse, or single-family home in the city, in the suburbs, or out in the country. Simply hold your breath until you hear them: wild birds. It is difficult to envision life without them.

AVIAN FEEDERS

After deciding to feed birds in your garden, there are a number of things to take into consideration.

Where would you like to view your birds? From a kitchen window, a sliding glass door leading to a deck, or a window on the second floor?

Pick a place that is simple to get to. You might be hesitant to fill a feeder that is not conveniently located next to a door or an easily accessible window during inclement weather, when birds are most susceptible. Additionally, choose a location where cleaning up bird droppings and abandoned seed shells won't be an issue.

Place your feeder out of the reach of the squirrels. When squirrels take control of a bird feeder, they cause a problem because they scare the birds away and scatter the seed all around. It is well known that squirrels can easily chew through wooden and plastic feeders.

It's fair to presume squirrels will visit your feeder if you've seen them in the area. Be very careful and thoughtful before hanging something from a tree limb. Because of their incredible agility, squirrels are likely to eat from any feeder that is hanging from a tree.

The least frustrating option in the long term is a squirrel-proof feeder or any feeder on a pole with a baffle. The pole-mounted metal "house" kind of feeder is the most effective squirrel-proof model.

What sort of bird food ought you to use? The most popular bird seed is sunflower. Cardinals, woodpeckers, blue jays, goldfinches, purple finches, chickadees, titmice, and nuthatches are among the species it draws. Obtain the black sunflower seeds, often known as "oil seeds." Birds prefer these seeds because they have more oil than the grey and white striped sunflower seeds found on the candy rack. They have softer shells, making it simpler to crack them apart. They are also less expensive than the grey and white ones.

Niger is yet another crucial bird seed. Niger is adored by goldfinches. Niger is a black seed that is so small and light that you can gently blow a handful of it away. Additionally, Niger costs over a dollar per pound, so you won't want to waste it. Purchase a hanging tube with tiny holes specifically made for Niger and put it where your best viewing window will let you see it. It's okay to set up near the home, even under the eaves. The goldfinches will become very tame and won't mind if you stand on the other side of the window, two feet away from them, while they are eating.

Safflower, a white seed that is somewhat smaller than a black sunflower seed, is also one of the birds' favorite seeds. The squirrels dislike it. Neither do starlings, blue jays, or grackles. Safflower seeds have a strong, bitter flavor. But since cardinals, titmice, chickadees, and downy woodpeckers eat it like candy, keep a plentiful supply on the platform feeder. The squirrels are also unwilling to climb up there.

Another seed that attracts birds is white millet. It is even more affordable than sunflower seeds. For the benefit of sparrows, juncos, and mourning doves, scatter it on the ground.

These seeds are available for purchase from feed shops, nurseries, supermarkets, and some hardware stores. Everything should be purchased in 50-pound bags, with the exception of the pricey niger, and kept in the garage in mouse-proof metal garbage cans.

Avoid buying mixed-seed packages for birds. These mixtures typically contain a lot of filler, including red millet. Most birds won't consume it. They dig through the seeds in the feeder and kick the red millet onto the ground, where it will, at the very least, remain until it rots and becomes quite good grass fertilizer. Mixed bird seed is not inexpensive.

Purchase the seeds that your birds will enjoy.

Be patient while beginning a feeding program. It could take as long as a few weeks before the birds find your feeders. As you wait, make sure to keep the feeders full. In due course, the birds will arrive.

Conscious people occasionally worry about whether feeding the birds may hurt them. Will the birds become reliant on the free food? And it's frequently suggested that one should start feeding birds only if they are certain that the feeding can go on uninterrupted.

The research suggests that feeding is not likely to be harmful to birds. They don't stick around and eat at just one establishment. According to studies of banded birds that can be individually identified, goldfinches, for instance, follow a circuit every day, stopping at several feeders and wild food patches.

Given that many households provide food for birds, it is unlikely that a bird will go hungry if one feeder runs out. However, birds that enter your yard at dusk are hungry, and it is impolite to disappoint visitors! Make sure they have enough to have a meal at your leisure.

Birds love to eat from hanging suet molds. You may buy these in many different places, but making them at home can be quite enjoyable. They are so simple that even kids can assist! Attach a small piece of rope to a pine cone, cover it with a suet, lard, or vegetable shortening combination (see below), wrap it in seeds, and dangle it from a tree branch to create a basic bird feeder.

Fatty combination: Mix 2 1/2 cups of cornmeal or uncooked oats with 1/2 cup of suet, lard, or vegetable shortening until thoroughly combined. Optionally, add 1/4 cup of finely chopped leftover meat, chopped nuts, or chopped dried fruit (only in cold weather).

Hummingbirds consume nectar, which is quite simple to manufacture on your own. Boiling water should be used to dissolve 1/4 cup of sugar. Place in your hummingbird feeder and wait for the birds to arrive! Change the nectar frequently because it can become rancid and hazardous for the birds, especially in warm weather. Additionally, hummingbirds typically like red nectar, so add a few drops of food colouring to the mixture!

Remind them to bring water! A bird bath is the best way to keep your feathered friends hydrated.

Backyard Bird Baths

Compassion in a birdbath. Your tiny circle of cold, clean water under a leafy tree is a favour to the birds because fresh, clean water is sometimes the most difficult thing for birds to obtain. It is also a courtesy to yourself and your family since you will find great joy in observing the birds at the birdbath.

A birdbath is actually one of the simplest ways to attract birds, so you can get a good look at them up close. Even more bird species can be attracted by water than by feeding.

Typically, seed-eaters like cardinals, blue jays, and sparrows are the target audience for bird feeders. Wrens, catbirds, and waxwings, which consume insects or fruit, typically don't find anything at the feeder to pique their attention. But every type of bird, from robins to screech owls, is drawn to the birdbath. Your understanding of the diversity of life will increase.

Commercial bird baths are sold in many budget shops, gardening supply stores, and home improvement centers, but you can create a birdbath out of just about anything.

Just make sure it provides the cool, pure water that birds most need.

What type of birdbath is ideal? It must be shallow—not more than three inches deep in the centre. Even shallower water should be present at the edge so that birds can easily enter. The majority of commercial birdbaths are too deep. If you already have a deep birdbath, you can add rocks to increase the depth, but doing so will make it slightly more difficult to maintain.

Consider installing a fountain or any other source of drip. Birds simply love the sound of falling water because it makes a plinking sound. It significantly boosts the variety of species that frequent birdbaths. Hummingbirds, for instance, would never wade into the bath like other birds because they only bathe while in flight. However, many people have observed hummingbirds flying back and forth across a birdbath's drips while timing their flights such that they catch a drop of water on each pass.

There are numerous ways to set up a drip. You can hang a bucket above the bath with a hole in the bottom that is 1/2 inch wide and a piece of cloth pushed into the hole to act as a wick, or run a horse so that it trickles into the water.

Make sure your bird bath has a rough bottom as well. Birds won't use a bath with a glazed, slippery bottom because they don't want to lose their balance. It's good to use cement. If you already have a slippery birdbath, you can cover it with the non-skid stickers that are offered for bathroom use.

Place your bird bath so that it can be seen from a window. Don't forget to include yourself in this photo. Place the birdbath somewhere indoors where you can see it, like your desk, dining room, or kitchen sink. Place the sink on a pedestal. It is simple to see from inside the house, simple to clean, and safer against predators. As an alternative, you might purchase a birdbath that hangs from a tree.

Placing your birdbath close enough for a hose to reach will make it simple to clean and refill. However, keep your birdbath away from your feeding station because seeds and droppings will quickly contaminate the water. Every few days, or even every day in hot weather, change the water. Dump it out or use the hose to squirt it out. Maintaining a scrub brush outside with your gardening tools will allow you to remove any potential algae growth.

Place the bird bath in an area where predators cannot get to your guests. Cats, for instance, like to wait behind bushes or other hiding objects before pouncing on birds when they are wet and struggling to fly. Therefore, situate your birdbath at least five to ten feet away from such hiding places. Give the birds an opportunity to spot the approaching cat. Give the birds a path of escape as well. The best place to hide is under some branches that are hanging down two or three feet from the bath. A wet bird can flutter one or two feet up to the shelter of the leaves.

Following these methods will result in a robin soon landing on the rim of your birdbath. He will dip his bill into the water before raising his head to allow the water to flow down his throat. He will then hop in and splash around wildly. He will let the water pour over his back after dousing his head with it. He will lounge around.

After he has finished bathing, he will fly to the nearest limb and shake off his feathers before preening them one by one through his bill.

A bird in the bath is the definition of joy. You will experience a burst of joy as soon as you catch a glimpse of it, even by accident through the window.

Homes for birds

You can decide that you don't want your birds to simply stop by to eat and take a bath every day. Maybe you'd like it if they stuck around for a while. Try erecting one or two birdhouses.

In the birdhouse industry, "one size fits all" is not a real concept. Choose the bird you want to attract, then buy a house for that specific species. You can find bird houses of many shapes and sizes, with or without perches, constructed of materials you might not have considered, such as recycled paper, gourds, plastic, rubber, pottery, metal, and concrete, by browsing any book or catalogue. A good birdhouse is created by utilizing the ideal blend of high-quality components and design.

The best building material for any birdhouse is wood. It is strong, provides decent insulation, and is breathable. Both red cedar and bald cypress should be at least three-quarters of an inch thick. Although they work, exterior-grade plywood and pine are less durable. No matter if the wood is a slab, rough-cut, or finished, as long as the interior hasn't been treated with stains or preservatives, it won't matter. The chemicals' fumes could hurt the birds.

The exterior of your birdhouse can be decorated however you like. Do you want your cardinals to roost in a clubhouse, or do you want your martins to hang out in a Victorian house?
As far as the outside of the house is concerned, anything goes. But don't give your birdhouse an aluminum roof. Birds will flee if the sun is shining directly in their eyes.

Make sure to provide drainage, ventilation, and simple access for upkeep and monitoring.

Your personal preferences will determine how elaborate your bird house is. The box's height, depth, floor measurements, diameter of the entrance hole, and height of the hole above the box floor are the most crucial factors to take into account in addition to where you place the box.

In bird boxes, air vents should be provided. There are two methods for providing ventilation:

Leave spaces between the roof and the box's sides or drill 1/4-inch holes right below the roof.

When water collects in a birdhouse's bottom, a problem arises. A roof with an adequate overhang and slope provides some protection. Additionally, drilling the entrance hole at an upward angle might help keep the water out. No matter how the design is done, driving rain will enter through the entrance hole. By rounding the corners of the box bottom and drilling 1/4-inch holes, you can ensure efficient drainage. If the floors are sunken by about 1/4 inch, nest boxes will last longer.

Look for the entrance hole at the top of the front panel. It is simpler for the adults to enter the box and, when the time comes, for the nestlings to climb out when there is a rough surface on the inside and outside.

Add a few grooves outside below the hole if your box is made of finished wood. Open the front panel and add cleats, wire mesh, or grooves to the interior. Never install a perch beneath a birdhouse's entrance hole.

Starlings, house sparrows, and other predators can easily wait for supper on perches. Avoid being seduced by duplexes or homes with more than one entrance hole. Cavity-nesting birds prefer not to share a home, with the exception of purple martins. These condos may seem lovely in your yard, but starlings and house sparrows are more likely to use them.

Your bird house's placement is just as crucial as its design and construction. Birds that nest in caverns are quite particular about their habitat. The birds are unlikely to find the house if you don't have the proper habitat. You can alter your property to attract the birds you want to see by adding a birdbath, fruit-bearing plants, more trees, or a pond with a waterfall.

Avoid placing bird houses next to bird feeders. Predators are less likely to harm dwellings that are installed on metal poles as opposed to those that are attached to tree trunks or hanging from tree branches.

Use no more than four tiny or one large nest box per acre for any one species. Put no more than one box in a tree unless it is really big or the boxes are for different species. If you experience extremely hot summers, face your boxes' entrance holes north or east to prevent the box from overheating.

You can even draw in some uncommon bird species by just beautifying your yard.

BIRDS' TERRAIN DESIGN

People may want to enhance their yard's "habitat" as they grow to appreciate the beauty of the birds that live nearby so that more birds will come to their property. We've already talked about enhancing their environment by installing birdhouses, feeders, and baths. Now let's consider how to grow different kinds of trees, shrubs, and flowers to entice birds. These can offer suitable nesting locations, winter protection, cover from predators, and year-round access to natural food sources.

Beautiful landscaping serves more purposes than just luring birds. It can raise the value of your home, provide natural beauty, and turn your yard into a children's playground as various animals are drawn to it.

Nine fundamental principles are involved in landscaping for birds:

Food

Every bird species has specific nutritional needs that may fluctuate as the seasons change. Find out what the birds you want to attract like to eat. To provide the fruits, berries, seeds, acorns, and nectar, establish the appropriate trees, shrubs, and flowers.

Water

By providing a supply of water, you might be able to double the variety of bird species that inhabit your yard. Birds will frequently use a frog pond, water garden, or bird bath, especially if the water is trickling, splashing, or flowing.

Shelter

Birds require locations where they may hide from predators and flee from bad weather. Excellent shelter can be found in trees (including dead ones), shrubs, long grass, and birdhouses.

Diversity

The best landscaping strategy is one that uses

a range of local species. The majority of bird species are drawn in by this.

The Four Seasons

Plant a variety of trees, shrubs, and flowers that will be beneficial all year to provide food and shelter for the birds.

Arrangement

Arrange the various habitat components in your yard properly. Take into account the impact of prevailing winds (and snow drifting) to safeguard your yard from harsh winter weather.

Protection

Birds should be shielded from needless death. Consider the accessibility of bird feeders and nest boxes to predators when deciding where to place them. Picture windows can also be a threat to birds. When they notice the reflections of trees and shrubs, they frequently fly directly toward windows.

On the outside of windows, a network of parallel, vertical strings spaced 4 inches apart can be installed to solve this issue. Be cautious while using certain pesticides and herbicides in your yard. Apply them only as necessary and strictly in accordance with the directions on the label. Try lawn care and gardening without using pesticides. The library's gardening books have more information.

Areas of hardiness

Consult a plant hardiness zone map, which can be purchased in most garden catalogues, before thinking about planting any non-native plants in your area. Make sure the plants you want are classified for your area's winter hardiness zone.

Topography and soils

To have your soil analyzed, speak with your neighborhood garden centre, university, or county extension office. Many plant species are adapted to particular types of soils. Knowing the type of soil you have will help you choose the plants that will thrive in your yard.

The following seven plant species are crucial as bird habitat:

Conifers

Conifers, which include pines, spruces, firs, arborvitae, junipers, cedars, and yews, are evergreen trees and shrubs. These plants provide a crucial role as winter refuge, summer breeding grounds, and escape cover. Some also provide fruits, seeds, and sap.

Legumes and Grass

Only if the land is not mowed during the nesting season can grasses and legumes provide shelter for ground-nesting birds. Some grasses and legumes also produce seeds. Native prairie grasses are gaining popularity as landscaping materials.

Plants That Produce Nectar

Nectar-producing plants are quite popular for luring orioles and hummingbirds. Hummingbirds find flowers with tubular red corollas to be especially alluring. Other trees, shrubs, vines, and flowers can also supply hummingbirds with nectar.

Seasonal fruiting plants

Plants in this category yield fruits or berries from May to August. These plants may attract brown thrashers, catbirds, robins, thrushes, waxwings, woodpeckers, orioles, cardinals, towhees, and grosbeaks throughout the summer months.

Several types of cherry, chokecherry, honeysuckle, raspberry, serviceberry, blackberry, blueberry, grape, mulberry, plum, and elderberry are examples of summer-fruiting plants.

Autumn-fruiting Plants

This landscape element consists of bushes and vines with fall-ripening fruit. These items are crucial for non-migratory species that need to eat in order to be ready for the winter season, as well as migratory birds that need to build up fat reserves before migration. Dogwoods, mountain ash, winterberries, cotton easters, and buffalo-berries are among the plants that bear fruit in the fall.

Winter-fruiting Plants

Winter-fruiting plants are those whose fruits continue to cling to the stems long after they first ripen in the fall. Many are unpalatable until they have been repeatedly frozen and thawed. Glossy black chokecherry, Siberian and "red magnificence" crabapples, snowberries, bittersweet, sumacs, American highbush cranberries, eastern and European wahoo, Virginia creeper, and Chinaberry are a few examples.

Acorn and nut plants

They consist of hazelnuts, oaks, hickories, buckeyes, chestnuts, butternuts, and walnuts. Numerous birds, including jays, woodpeckers, and titmice, consume the meat from cracked nuts and acorns. These plants also help to provide suitable nesting habitat.

How do you begin now that you have this extensive understanding of plants that attract birds? Your aim will be to establish a variety of bird-attracting trees, shrubs, and flowers. If you carefully plan, it may be both affordable and enjoyable for the entire family.

Establish your priorities first. Choose the types of birds you want to attract, and then design your plan around their requirements. Ask your friends and neighbors what sorts of birds frequent your neighborhood to learn more. Attend a meeting of the local bird club and ask local birdwatchers how they manage to draw birds to their yards.

Use local plants whenever it is possible. For listings of trees, shrubs, and wildflowers that are indigenous to your area, check with the botany department of a nearby college or university or your state's natural heritage program. Use this list as the basis for your landscape design.

These plants are a wise long-term investment because they are naturally adapted to the climate in your area. Many native plants are gorgeous for landscaping and fantastic for birds. Make sure that any common plant species you include in your design are not what plant experts would refer to as "invasive pests." Look through the bird books at your neighborhood library.

Draw a map of your land as a starting point. Sketch the plants you want to add to your map. Draw shrubs at their full mature breadth and trees at a scale that represents three-fourths of their mature width. This will assist you in determining how many trees and plants you need.

There is a tendency to include so many trees that your yard will soon be completely shaded. Make sure to leave bright, open areas for flowers and shrubs to grow. Determine the amount of money you may spend and the duration of your project. Try not to try to do too much at once. Consider implementing a five-year development plan.

Review the seven plant parts that were previously described. Which elements are already present? Which ones are absent? Keep in mind that you are attempting to provide food and shelter through all four seasons. Make a list of the plants you believe will provide the missing habitat elements.

Finally, get started! Start your plants and involve your entire family so they can feel good about helping the wildlife. Record your plants using paper and photos. Try photographing your yard from the same locations each year to track the development of your plants.

Keep your garden looking fantastic. Use landscape film, wood chips, or shredded bark mulch to keep your planting areas weed-free and to properly water your new trees, shrubs, and flowers. Herbicides are not used in this method to control weeds. Consult a local nursery, garden centre, or county extension agent if issues arise with your plants.

Watching Birds at Night

Most backyard bird watchers believe that the bird population becomes active in the early morning, but you may be pleasantly surprised to hear that a significant portion of the bird population becomes active as the sun sets. When night falls, nocturnal birds get ready for their regular activities, such as eating. So get your flashlights ready for some truly fascinating night bird watching that isn't your typical backyard gazing.

Most backyard bird watchers believe that the bird population becomes active in the early morning, but you may be pleasantly surprised to hear that a sizable portion of the bird population becomes active as the sun sets. When night falls, nocturnal birds get ready for their regular routines, including eating. So get your flashlights ready for some really fascinating birding and go on a nighttime bird viewing excursion.

Before you leap right into the realm of night bird watching, it is a good idea to become familiar with the location you will be visiting. Avoiding unknown regions in the dark is always a smart idea, if only to prevent getting lost or injured. Recall that it is dark.

A powerful flashlight is the item you should bring with you most of all. The use of a red lens is essential for seeing animals at night. A yellow light will act as a deterrent and cause all of your viewing subjects to flee if you attempt to use one. Their eyes are harmed by yellow light just as much as yours are. On the other hand, red light does not cause the pupils to dilate and does not irritate the eye, causing the objects you are watching to remain still as if nothing were happening. If you don't have a red lens, wrapping a piece of red plastic around the flashlight's end will do.

When you go out at night to do some bird watching, you should be aware that other animals will be present, as birds are not the only nocturnal animals. This is not your garden, and you are not seated nearby admiring a tube bird feeder. Enjoy the wonderful sounds of the evening while using your handy flashlight to spot any other animals that may be darting about. The best way to find the nightlife is to simply remain in one place.

After observing birds in the evening for a while, you will start to grow accustomed to the noises of the night. The cricket and bug noises will fade away, and the twig snaps and coyote howls that once terrified you will become part of the serene background noise of a wonderful bird watching experience. It will be just as delightful to experience nature at night as it is to spend the mornings in the backyard with your coffee and newspaper while watching your tube bird feeder.

Final Words

Although it is not the simplest activity in the world to learn, birding is undoubtedly one of the most enjoyable. There will be many years' worth of enjoyable and interesting field trips to make up for those first adventures when you glanced through your field guide in frustration.

Every time a birder goes out, you may see them encountering something new. Even if they don't discover a new species, they might observe novel behavior, hear novel vocalizations, or simply discover a novel and wild area of Florida. They may even come across something shocking, such as a rare European bird that has somehow wandered off course.

Birdwatching has two major draws: its constant variety and difficulty, but it also has a social component. In the United States, some 42 million people enjoy casual bird watching, feeding, and monitoring birds near their homes. Only about 17 million people travel specifically to observe birds. Still, that's a lot of people craning their necks upward and thrusting their heads into bushes. Birding is constantly surrounded by a universe of fresh acquaintances and novel encounters.

Beginning birding will have its frustrating moments, but if you give it a decent shot and understand the fundamentals, you'll soon get obsessed!

Bird watching is a quest. You set out to see birds, but what you return with can only be described as bliss. Being able to identify birds is like having a lifetime pass to the natural world's theatre.

If you're a newbie, it's crucial to keep in mind that the more time you spend observing the birds, the more you will come to appreciate them. Don't be discouraged by the typical jokes from friends or coworkers (yes, there will still be some people who won't understand why you are captivated by birds); just do it and wow everyone around you!

To all, happy birdwatching!

About The Author

Leigh Watson is an avid Birdwatcher and ornithologist. From an early age, he observed and sketched birds, and during the 1980s and 1990s, he travelled extensively across North America in pursuit of birds. He is a well-known speaker around the world, and his writing has appeared in a number of print and online magazines, including the Washington Post, Outdoor News, Birds & Blooms, 10,000 Birds, and Audubon.